# The Giant Turtle

大ㄉㄚˋ龜ㄍㄨㄟ王ㄨㄤˊ

Published, translated, and adapted by the
Buddhist Text Translation Society
Dharma Realm Buddhist University
Dharma Realm Buddhist Association
Burlingame, California U.S.A.

翻ㄈㄢ譯ㄧˋ：佛ㄈㄛˊ經ㄐㄧㄥ翻ㄈㄢ譯ㄧˋ委ㄨㄟˇ員ㄩㄢˊ會ㄏㄨㄟˋ

出ㄔㄨ版ㄅㄢˇ：法ㄈㄚˋ界ㄐㄧㄝˋ佛ㄈㄛˊ教ㄐㄧㄠˋ總ㄗㄨㄥˇ會ㄏㄨㄟˋ／佛ㄈㄛˊ經ㄐㄧㄥ翻ㄈㄢ譯ㄧˋ委ㄨㄟˇ員ㄩㄢˊ會ㄏㄨㄟˋ／法ㄈㄚˋ界ㄐㄧㄝˋ佛ㄈㄛˊ教ㄐㄧㄠˋ大ㄉㄚˋ學ㄒㄩㄝˊ

**The Giant Turtle**

A fictionalized version of " The Tortoise King, " Human Roots,
Buddhist Text Translation Society, 1982.
Illustrations by Candy, age 9, with a little help from her friends.


Published by:
Buddhist Text Translation Society
1777 Murchison Drive
Burlingame, California 94010-4504


(c) 2000_ Buddhist Text Translation Society
          Dharma Realm Buddhist University
          Dharma Realm Buddhist Association


First bilingual Chinese/English edition 2000

09 08 07 06 05 04 03 02 01 00       10 9 8 7 6 5 4 3 2 1

Printed in Taiwan, R.O.C.

Addresses of the Dharma Realm Buddhist Association branches are
listed at the back of this book.


Library of Congress Cataloging-in-Publication Data

The giant turtle = / Published and translated and adapted by the Buddhist Text
Translation Society = [Ta chu kuei] / Fan i Fo ching fan i wei yuan hui.
      p. cm. -- (Yu liang ts ' ung shu ; CE001)
Parallel title in Chinese characters.
Summary: In a past life, Shakyamuni Buddha was a huge turtle who crawled onto the
beach for a nap and was mistaken for a mountain by people who built their homes and
shops on his back.
  ISBN 0-88139-850-0 (pbk. : alk. paper)
    1. Jataka stories, English. 2. Tipioaka. Suttapioaka. Khuddakanikaya.
Jataka-Paraphrases, English. [1. Jataka stories. 2. Chinese language
materials-Bilingual.] I. Title: [Ta chu kuei]. II. Buddhist Text Translation Society. III.
Series.


  BQ1462.E5 G53 2000
  294.3 ' 82325--dc21

                                                                99-088878

# The Giant Turtle

大龜王

## Jataka Tales

The Jataka tales are stories that the Buddha told about the many times he was reborn on Earth, sometimes as a prince or a poor man, sometimes as an animal or a fish or a tree. These stories celebrate the wonderful joy, compassion, wisdom, and kindness that the Buddha showed in each of these lives to help others.

The Giant Turtle is one of the tales told by the Buddha to his disciples over 2,500 years ago.

## 前言

Jakata tales是佛陀述說自己前生的故事，他有時生為太子或窮人，有時就做動物或魚，乃至一棵樹。這些故事稱頌著佛陀，在其每一生幫助人時，所表現出來的圓妙喜悅、慈悲、智慧與仁慈。這篇「大龜王」是二千五百年前，佛陀告訴弟子的故事之一。

# The Giant Turtle

Once a long, long time ago, the Buddha came to the earth as a giant turtle. He was a king turtle and ruled over all the animals in the deep blue sea. Every day he swam among the painted fish, the pearly-white oysters, and the blue whales, helping them with their problems and wishing them well. Everyone was happy and peaceful in his kingdom of the sea.

# 大龜王

很久很久以前，佛陀化身為一隻大龜王，來統領藍海中所有的水族。牠每天在五彩繽紛的魚、珍珠白的蛤蜊，及藍藍的海鯨間游來游去，除了幫牠們解決問題外，還希望牠們事事如意；所以一切的水族，都在牠的王國裏，過著既快樂、又祥和的生活。

5

One day, he crawled onto the sandy beach to take a nap. Because he was so large, as large as a continent, he napped for a very long time, for thousands of years.

有一天牠爬到沙灘上小睡片刻。可是牠實在太大了，大得好像一片陸地一樣，所以這一睡，竟睡了一千年這麼長的時間！

In the nights, the rain came dropping tiny raindrops onto the turtle's back. Drip, drop! Drip, drop! The raindrops flowed down between the cracks on the turtle's great shell, forming sparkling rivers and lakes.

The turtle slept on.

夜晚，小雨滴在大龜王的背上，滴答！滴答！雨滴流進了牠巨大龜殼的縫隙中，形成了亮晶晶的河流和湖泊；可是大龜王還是沉睡著。

In the mornings, the winds came up, blowing tiny grains of sand onto the turtle's back. Whoo-sha! Whoo-sha! The grains of sand joined together forming mountains and valleys.

The turtle slept on.

早上，風把細沙吹到大龜王的背上，呼嚕！呼嚕！沙粒堆在一起，形成了山嶺和峽谷；可是大龜王還是沉睡著。

In the afternoons, the birds flew over, dropping tiny seeds onto the turtle's back. Pi-link! Pi-link! The seeds sprouted, and there on the turtle's back grew flowers and grass and trees.

The turtle slept on.

午間，飛鳥銜落的小種子掉到大龜王的背上，嗶剝！嗶剝！種子在龜背上發了芽，長出花草樹木來；可是大龜王還是沉睡著。

The sun warmed the turtle through the days.

白天，陽光溫暖了大龜王；

The moon watched over him through the nights.

夜晚，月光映照著牠。

As time passed, the seasons embraced the giant turtle with Spring, Summer, Autumn, and Winter, and animals that lived on the turtle's back experienced the seasons and multiplied.

時間一天一天地過去了，春、夏、秋、冬四季輪流擁抱著大龜王，動物們也來住在牠的背上，度過了四季，並且數量一天天地增加。

One day, not knowing the difference between the earth and the giant turtle's back, a child drifted among the mountains and valleys to pick some wild flowers.

有<sub>ㄧㄡˇ</sub>一<sub>ㄧ</sub>天<sub>ㄊㄧㄢ</sub>，一<sub>ㄧ</sub>位<sub>ㄨㄟˋ</sub>無<sub>ㄨˊ</sub>法<sub>ㄈㄚˇ</sub>分<sub>ㄈㄣ</sub>辨<sub>ㄅㄧㄢˋ</sub>土<sub>ㄊㄨˇ</sub>地<sub>ㄉㄧˋ</sub>和<sub>ㄏㄜˊ</sub>龜<sub>ㄍㄨㄟ</sub>背<sub>ㄅㄟˋ</sub>的<sub>ㄉㄜ˙</sub>小<sub>ㄒㄧㄠˇ</sub>女<sub>ㄋㄩˇ</sub>孩<sub>ㄏㄞˊ</sub>，在<sub>ㄗㄞˋ</sub>山<sub>ㄕㄢ</sub>谷<sub>ㄍㄨˇ</sub>間<sub>ㄐㄧㄢ</sub>漫<sub>ㄇㄢˋ</sub>遊<sub>ㄧㄡˊ</sub>，採<sub>ㄘㄞˇ</sub>了<sub>ㄌㄜ˙</sub>一<sub>ㄧ</sub>些<sub>ㄒㄧㄝ</sub>野<sub>ㄧㄝˇ</sub>花<sub>ㄏㄨㄚ</sub>。

The next day she returned with her family. "This will be a good place to build a house. We can grow rice and get salt from the sea," said her father.

The turtle slept on.

第二天，她帶著家人又來了，她的父親說：「這是一片可以建造家園的好土地，我們不但可以在這兒種稻，還可以從海裏採鹽哩！」可是大龜王還是沉睡著。

The next year another family moved to the little mountain, and then another.

過了一年，另一個家庭又搬進小山，接著其他的家庭也陸續搬來了。

Roads were built and merchants came to set up shops.

這時，馬路被造起來了，商人也來設立商店。

A prince even built a palace.

The turtle slept on.

有一位王子甚至建立了一座宮殿！

可是大龜王還是沉睡著。

People pulled their carts and rode their carriages over the streets cutting deep ruts into the turtle's shell. Their cities became a heavy burden on his back, and the noises they made drummed in his ears. The fires that they built for their needs burned his skin.

人們在馬路上開車騎馬，車轍深深地切進了龜殼內；他們的城市重重地壓在牠的背上；人們的吵雜聲，如捶鼓似地傳入了牠的耳朵；他們所燃的火，更是燒透了牠的殼！

And so it went until one day the giant turtle was awakened by the pain from the fires. He wanted to cool himself, so he began to crawl toward the sea. He did not hear the people cry, "Earthquake! Earthquake!" or see them run hither and yon.

所以有一天，大龜王從燒灼的痛苦中醒來了，牠想要涼快自己，就開始往海裏爬。但是牠沒聽到人們哭喊著：「地震！地震！」也沒看到人們四處狂奔著。

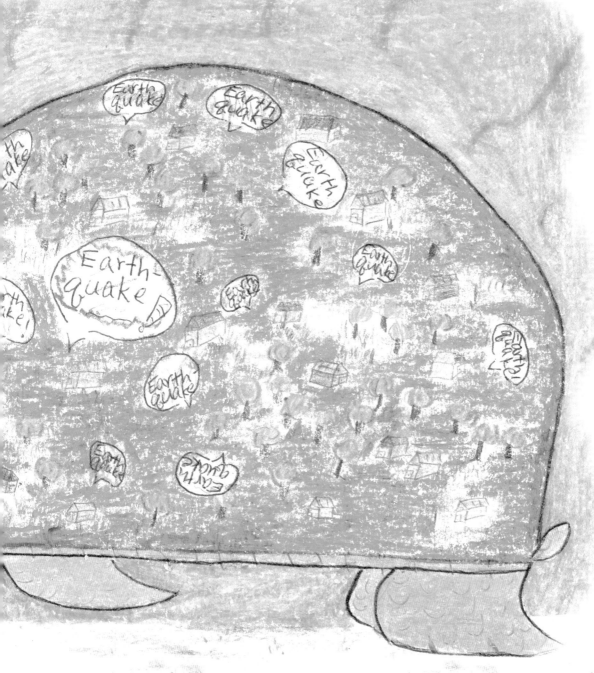

When the giant turtle reached the sea, he immersed himself
in the cool water to ease his pain. As the dwellers on his
back saw water rising all around them, they screamed,
"Flood! Flood! We will drown!"

當大龜王回到海裏時，牠將自己浸
在冷水中，以解除痛苦；而牠背上
的居民一看到水漲到身邊，都尖叫
起來：「洪水！洪水！我們快淹死
了。」

For the first time, the giant turtle realized that there were people living on his back. Not wanting to bring pain into their lives, he crawled back onto the beach.

這一次， 大龜王總算知道有人住在牠的背上了！ 為了不給人們帶來痛苦， 牠又爬回海灘上。

For another thousand years, he let the fires burn his skin and the rumble of the city shake him. During the days he held back the tears, but in the night he let them flow. So great was his pain and so silent were his tears that no one knew of his sacrifice.

另一個一千年又過去了，牠還是任由火燒灼著牠，任由城市隆隆的聲音震動著牠。白天牠的淚水往內吞，晚間則讓淚水靜靜地流下來。牠的痛苦是如此的巨大，可是牠的淚水卻如此的無聲無息，以致於沒有人知道牠的犧牲。

Finally the giant turtle decided that he needed to return to the sea. Slowly raising his head, he spoke to the people, "Do not be afraid. I will not hurt you. You see, I am a giant turtle, and you are living on my shell. I must go back into the water, or I will die."

One by one, the people gathered their belongings and moved back onto the beach. The giant turtle eased their buildings and homes and palaces off his back. The people created new villages and cities on the earth, and their lives went on as before.

最後，大龜王決定牠必須回到海裏去，所以慢慢地抬起頭來對人們說：「不要害怕！我不會傷害你們的。你看！我是一隻巨大的烏龜，可是你們卻住在我的背殼上；現在我必須回到水裏，否則我會死的。」

這時，人們一個接一個收拾他們的財物，然後搬到岸上。當背上的建築物、家園、宮殿被除去後，大龜王也感到舒服了。人們在陸地上建立了新的村落和城市，就如同以前一樣地過日子。

All were grateful for the kindness of the giant turtle. They bowed to him, saying, " For thousands of years, you gave us your back on which to build our world, and now you save our lives. You are king turtle! Surely, you will become a Buddha in the future."

大龜王的慈悲，令大家都非常感激，人們禮拜牠說：「數千年來，你讓我們在你的背上建立我們的世界，現在還救了我們的生命，你真是一位王者呀！將來一定會成佛的！」

Then the birds flew high above the turtle and placed garlands of fragrant flowers around his neck. Monkeys rubbed his sores with healing herbs, and elephants trumpeted sweet music to soothe his ears.

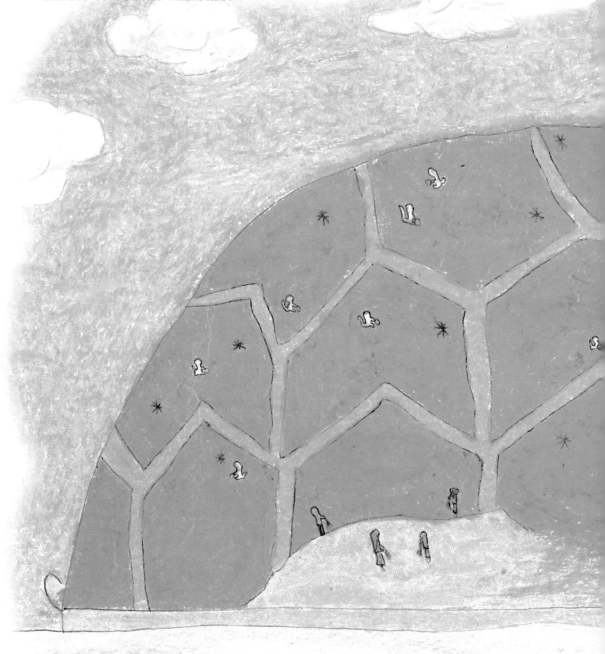

接著鳥兒也來到牠的上空飛翔，將香花鬘掛在牠的頸子上；猴子們用了藥草來幫牠敷癒傷口；大象們豎起長鼻子，奏著甜美的音樂，來撫慰牠的耳朵。

The people swept the sand from his back with peacock
feathers, and the giant turtle crawled back into the sea.

人們則拿著孔雀的羽毛掃除了牠背
上的沙；　最後大龜王又回到海裏
了！

48

After the telling of this tale, the Buddha said, "I was the king turtle and the people who lived on my back became my disciples."

講完了這個故事後，佛陀就說：「我就是那隻大龜王，那些住在我背上的人，後來就變成我的弟子。」

# 法界佛教總會簡介
## The Dharma Realm Buddhist Association

法界佛教總會是上宣下化老和尚，於一九五九年在美國創立。本會是以法界爲體；以將佛教的眞實義理，傳播到世界各地爲目的；以翻譯經典、弘揚正法、提倡道德教育、利樂一切有情爲己任。本著上人所創的六大宗旨：不爭、不貪、不求、不自私、不自利、不妄語，奉行：凍死不攀緣，餓死不化緣，窮死不求緣，隨緣不變，不變隨緣，抱定我們三大宗旨；捨命爲佛事，造命爲本事，正命爲僧事，即事明理，明理即事，推行祖師一脈心傳。

數十年來，法總陸續成立了金山聖寺、萬佛聖城、法界聖城等國際性道場多處。其中僧眾均須恪遵佛制，秉持日中一食、衣不離體之家風，持戒念佛，習教參禪，和合共住，獻身佛教。此外本會並設有國際譯經學院、僧伽居士訓練班、法界佛教大學及中、小學等機構，以推展譯經及教育工作。

本會所屬之道場、機構，門戶開放，沒有人我、國籍、宗教之分，凡各國各教人士，願致力於仁義道德、明心見性者，皆歡迎前來共同研究，修持學習。

The Dharma Realm Buddhist Association (DRBA) was founded by the Venerable Master Hsuan Hua in the United States of America in 1959 to bring the genuine teachings of the Buddha to the entire world. Its goals are to propagate the Proper Dharma, to translate the Mahayana Buddhist scriptures into the world's languages and to promote ethical education. The members of the Association guide themselves with six ideals established by the Venerable Master which are: no fighting, no greed, no seeking, no selfishness, no pursuing personal advantage, and no lying. They hold in mind the credo:

*Freezing, we do not scheme.*

*Starving, we do not beg.*

*Dying of poverty, we ask for nothing.*

*According with conditions, we do not change.*

*Not changing, we accord with conditions.*

*We adhere firmly to our three great principles.*

*We renounce our lives to do the Buddha's work.*

*We take responsibility in molding our own destinies.*

*We rectify our lives to fulfill our role as members of the Sangha.*

*Encountering specific matters, we understand the principles.*

*Understanding the principles, we apply them in specific matters.*

*We carry on the single pulse of the patriarchs' mind-transmission.*

During the decades that followed DRBA's establishment, international Buddhist communities such as Gold Mountain Monastery, the City of Ten Thousand Buddhas, the City of the Dharma Realm, and various other branch facilities were founded. All these operate under the traditions of the Venerable Master and through the auspices of the Dharma Realm Buddhist Association. Following the Buddhas' guidelines, the Sangha members in these monastic facilities maintain the practices of taking only one meal a day and of always wearing their precept sashes. Reciting the Buddha's name, studying the teachings, and practicing meditation, they dwell together in harmony and personally put into practice Shakyamuni Buddha's teachings. Reflecting Master Hua's emphasis on translation and education, the Association also sponsors an International Translation Institute, vocational training programs for Sangha and laity, Dharma Realm Buddhist University, and elementary and secondary schools.

The Way-places of this Association are open to sincere individuals of all races, religions, and nationalities. Everyone who is willing to put forth his or her best effort in nurturing humaneness, righteousness, merit, and virtue in order to understand the mind and see the nature is welcome to join in the study and practice.

法界佛教總會・萬佛聖城

**Dharma Realm Buddhist Association**

**The City of Ten Thousand Buddhas**

2001 Talmage Road, Talmage, CA 95481-0217 U.S.A.

Tel: (707) 462-0939   Fax: (707) 462-0949

• • • • • • • • • • • • • • • • • • • • • • • • • • • • • • • • • • • • • • • • • • • • • • • • • • • •

國際譯經學院 **The International Translation Institute**

1777 Murchison Drive, Burlingame, CA 94010-4504 U.S.A.

Tel: (650) 692-5912   Fax: (650) 692-5056

法界宗教研究院（柏克萊寺）

**Institute for World Religions (at Berkeley Buddhist Monastery)**

2304 McKinley Avenue, Berkeley, CA 94703 U.S.A.

Tel: (510) 848-3440   Fax: (510) 548-4551

金山聖寺 **Gold Mountain Monastery**

800 Sacramento Street, San Francisco, CA 94108 U.S.A.

Tel: (415) 421-6117   Fax: (415) 788-6001

金聖寺 **Gold Sage Monastery**

11455 Clayton Road, San Jose, CA 95127 U.S.A.

Tel: (408) 923-7243   Fax: (408) 923-1064

法界聖城 **The City of the Dharma Realm**

1029 West Capitol Avenue, West Sacramento, CA 95691 U.S.A.

Tel/Fax: (916) 374-8268

金輪聖寺 **Gold Wheel Monastery**

235 North Avenue 58, Los Angeles, CA 90042 U.S.A.

Tel/Fax: (323) 258-6668

長堤聖寺 **Long Beach Monastery**

3361 East Ocean Boulevard, Long Beach, CA 90803 U.S.A.

Tel/Fax: (562) 438-8902

福祿壽聖寺 **Blessings, Prosperity, and Longevity Monastery**

4140 Long Beach Boulevard, Long Beach, CA 90807 U.S.A.

Tel/Fax: (562) 595-4966

華嚴精舍 **Avatamsaka Hermitage**

11721 Beall Mountain Road, Potomac, MD 20854-1128 U.S.A.

Tel/Fax: (301) 299-3693

金峰聖寺 **Gold Summit Monastery**

233 First Avenue West, Seattle, WA 98119 U.S.A.

Tel/Fax: (206) 217-9320

金佛聖寺 **Gold Buddha Monastery**

301 East Hastings Street, Vancouver, BC V6A 1P3 Canada

Tel/Fax: (604) 684-3754

華嚴聖寺 **Avatamsaka Monastery**

1009 Fourth Avenue S.W., Calgary, AB T2P 0K8 Canada

Tel/Fax: (403) 234-0644

法界佛教印經會 **Dharma Realm Buddhist Books Distribution Society**

臺灣省臺北市忠孝東路六段85號11樓

11th Floor, 85 Chung-hsiao E. Road, Sec. 6, Taipei, R.O.C.

Tel: (02) 2786-3022, 2786-2474　Fax: (02) 2786-2674

法界聖寺 **Dharma Realm Sage Monastery**

臺灣省高雄縣六龜鄉興龍村東溪山莊20號

20, Tung-hsi Shan-chuang, Hsing-lung Village, Liu-kuei, Kaohsiung County, Taiwan, R.O.C.

Tel: (07) 689-3713　Fax: (07) 689-3870

彌陀聖寺 **Amitabha Monastery**

臺灣省花蓮縣壽豐鄉池南村四健會7號

7, Su-chien-hui, Chih-nan Village, Shou-feng, Hualien County, Taiwan, R.O.C.

Tel: (03) 865-1956　Fax:(03) 865-3426

紫雲洞觀音寺 **Tze Yun Tung Temple**

Batu 5 1/2, Jalan Sungai Besi, Salak Selatan, 57100 Kuala Lumpur, Malaysia

Tel: (03)782-6560　Fax:(03) 780-1272

蓮華精舍 **Lotus Vihara**

136, Jalan Sekolah, 45600 Batang Berjuntai, Selangor Darul Ehsan, Malaysia

Tel: (03) 871-9439

登彼岸觀音堂 **Deng Bi An Temple**

161, Jalan Ampang, 50450 Kuala Lumpur, Malaysia

Tel: (03) 2164-8055　Fax: (03)2163-7118

佛教講堂 **Buddhist Lecture Hall**

香港跑馬地黃泥涌道31號12樓

31 Wong Nei Chong Road, Top Floor, Happy Valley, Hong Kong

Tel/Fax: 2572-7644

# 大ㄉㄚ龜ㄍㄨㄟ王ㄨㄤ

西曆二〇〇〇年一月十四日・育良叢書ICE001
佛曆三〇二五年十二月初八日・釋迦牟尼佛成道日・初版

發行人　法界佛教總會
出　版　法界佛教總會・佛經翻譯委員會・法界佛教大學
地　址　**Dharma Realm Buddhist Association &**
　　　　**The City of Ten Thousand Buddhas**
　　　　2001 Talmage Road, Talmage, CA 95481-0217 U.S.A.
　　　　電話: (707) 462-0939　傳眞: (707) 462-0949

**The International Translation Institute**
1777 Murchison Drive, Burlingame, CA 94010-4504 U.S.A.
電話: (650) 692-5912　傳眞: (650) 692-5056

插畫者　小糖糖 (Candy)
倡　印　萬佛聖城
　　　　The City of Ten Thousand Buddhas
　　　　2001 Talmage Road, Talmage, CA 95481-0217 USA
　　　　電話: (707) 462-0939　傳眞: (707) 462-0949

ISBN 0-88139-850-0